BOYS WITH PLANTS

- 50 Boys and the Plants They Love -

Curated by Scott Cain

CHRONICLE BOOKS
SAN FRANCISCO

CONTENTS

INTRODUCTION 4

Choosing the right plant for you 5

Keeping your plant alive 6

THE BOYS AND THEIR PLANTS 8

Aaron	@_moose_____	10
AJ	@savereign	12
Alan	@plant.jungle	14
Alexander	@alexander.hoyle	16
Anders	@arcticgardener	18
Ben	@bennguyendesign	20
Bernat	@bernatamate	22
Blendi	@balajblendi	24
Bryson	@brysonjmosley	26
Budi	@darmawandii	28
Cody	@codyraptorowens	30
Corentin	@corentinpfeifferfleuriste	32
Cory	@corypaul2	34
Dabito	@dabito	36

Emil	@thelimelife_	38	**Muhammed**	@behind_the_seeds	78
Glenn	@glenn.arvor	40	**Mykie**	@mykier	80
Goof	@goofkloosterman	42	**Nick**	@nickotene	82
Igor	@igorjosif	44	**Olle**	@upleafting	84
James B	@baetanical	46	**Oskar**	@plantthatplant	86
James I	@jamesipy	48	**Patrick**	@copperplants	88
Jamie	@jamies_jungle	50	**Pierluigi**	@hyperdecadence	90
Jan K	@homebyfousna	52	**Raymond**	@mustybooks	92
Jan R	@jarobin_	54	**Remigiusz**	@warsawjungle	94
John	@delapa1	56	**Ronnie**	@ohsummossum	96
Jon	@jongomezdelap	58	**Shabi**	@fiori_tlv	98
Jonathan	@jrlefrancois	60	**Thiago**	@thiagovicenteoliveira	100
Jono	@jono.fleming	62	**Travis**	@no_curtisy	102
Luca	@luca.iaco	64	**Tyrell**	@gothaigo	104
Mark	@mrk.gif	66	**Zack**	@zack_bez	106
Martin	@martinehmele	68	**Zaki**	@zqqyjml	108
Maurício	@maujorge	70			
Mert	@mrtzldg	72			
Michael	@houseofhortus	74			
Mihalis	@mihalisnyc	76			

INTRODUCTION

Boys with Plants began in Perth, Australia. I have a passion for house plants and a very large balcony full of them, and a few years ago I started sharing photos of these plants on my Instagram account, *TropicaLoco*.

Scott Cain   Photo: Dennis Tan

I was amazed at how popular these photos became and through the account I met a community of plant-lovers, including James (see page 48) from Singapore. James and I started discussing our plant finds, how much sunlight a *Pilea* needs, and which pot best goes with which plant. We also started sharing photos of handsome men and their plants—which inspired me to start the Boys with Plants Instagram account.

I should have known that an account about boys and plants would find an audience, but I couldn't have anticipated this. It's been so exciting to watch the account grow. I've particularly enjoyed reading all the comments on the posts and seeing the media buzz.

I was thrilled at the opportunity to create this beautiful book, and I hope you enjoy flipping through it as much as I loved putting it together!

Scott Cain
@boyswithplants

Choosing the right plant for you

You stroll into your local plant shop in search of the perfect plant for your home. What do you look for? Which plant is right for you?

If you're new to house plants, you might like to start with one of the Top 10 "hard-to-killables" (see page 6). They're fairly easy to keep alive and will look great in any interior. When I choose a new plant I go for variety. Light and feathery or sharp and spiky. Neon to deep emerald green as well as pink, purple and deep velvety black.

But before getting too carried away, look carefully and examine your new plant's health. Sad, wilted leaves or soil that is powdery and dry might be a sign your plant hasn't been well looked after. Also, a mealybug outbreak would not be the house addition that you had in mind! It's worth having a chat with the charming, bearded guy behind the counter to find out exactly what your new plant's needs are.

Next you'll need to match the plant with a planter. Will the plant be the hero or will it be the pot? You could

Anders p. 18

go with brightly glazed ceramic, self-watering polypropylene, or classic terracotta, but also consider a vintage planter, a cane basket, or a macramé hanger to show off plants with long-hanging tendrils.

Good luck and have fun choosing the perfect plant for you!

Keeping your plant alive

Now that you've brought your perfect plant home, you're going to want to keep it alive!

Fortunately most plants sold as house plants are fairly adaptable to indoor conditions. Each individual variety has its own quirks, and it's worth doing a bit of research to find out what they are.

Indoor plants usually thrive in bright, indirect light. While there are some varieties that will survive in low-light conditions, a rule-of-thumb is that if it's comfortable light to read in, your indoor plants will love it.

You can't always rely on the soil that the plant comes in, as it can be unsuitable for helping your plant have a long and healthy life. Investing in a good quality potting medium will really help your plant's roots thrive.

Indoor plants generally prefer warm, steady temperatures, which means that drafty positions or sharp changes can be very damaging. Tropical plants like humidity, which you can increase by grouping plants together to create a happy little microclimate.

One way that new plant lovers kill their new plants is over-watering. There's no set schedule, but if you wriggle your finger into the soil and find it's completely dry, it's time to give your plants a splash of water. Most plants don't like sitting in saucers of water either, so try putting some pebbles in the tray to lift your plants up. This will help increase the humidity around your plant too.

Remember, even the most experienced plant lover has killed a plant or two. Just try and learn from your mistakes and they'll thrive!

Top 10 "hard-to-killables"

- *Sansevieria*
- *Hoya*
- *Ficus elastica*
- Cast iron plant
- *Zamioculcas zamiifolia*
- Devil's ivy
- Peace lily
- *Tradescantia zebrina*
- *Dracaena fragrans*
- *Monstera deliciosa*

Remigiusz p. 94

THE BOYS AND THEIR PLANTS

Aaron

📷 **@_moose_____**

👦 **Aaron Warnecke, 28, American**

📍 **Philadelphia, Pennsylvania, USA**

ⓘ To investment banker Aaron, size does count—he thinks the bigger the plant, the better! Aaron has turned his warehouse apartment into an urban jungle, filling the space with big leafy plants like *Monstera deliciosa* and fiddle-leaf figs. He's lucky enough to be able to control the levels of light in his home, making his plants easier to care for.

Aaron says: *"Adding plants to your home creates an environment of stillness and peace. I like to be surrounded by plants as I conduct my yoga practice, it really makes it magical."*

❝ *'Leaf' humans and plants better than you found them.*

AJ

@savereign

AJ Arellano, 27, Filipino

Greenville, South Carolina, USA

As a professional plant stylist, AJ spends a lot of his time with plants. His favorites are large, leafy varieties like the dragon tree or slightly unworldly types like the staghorn fern. While AJ's care tips include misting his plants thoroughly and regularly playing them music, stylistically he likes to adapt his space to his frondy friends, imagining how bookshelves, cabinets, and even the shower can be adapted to complement different plant specimens.

AJ says: *"Some people love the look of plants but tend not to give them the care they need. That said, do not get intimidated by labor intensive plants! Take chances! Plants that don't work for some people and are deemed 'difficult' might just work for you."*

> " *Make sure you do your research on the plant you are thinking about buying.*

Alan

📷 **@plant.jungle**

🧒 **Alan Chan, 27, Australian**

📍 **Sydney, New South Wales, Australia**

ℹ️ Alan is a man of various trades; not only a plant stylist, he's also a digital content creator and a teacher. He is minutely attentive to the light and water requirements of each of his plants; once he has ascertained how much they like to drink and sunbathe, he then accessorizes them with a range of colorful and monochromatic pots and plant stands.

Alan says: *"When we're out for the day, our plants love to talk and gossip. Place your plants together; it helps increase humidity and creates a mini-ecosystem if you cluster plants with similar growth patterns and the same light requirements."*

“ *Plants are happiest when they get to hang out with their friends!*

Alexander

📷 **@alexander.hoyle**

👦 **Alexander Hoyle, 24, British**

📍 **London, UK**

💬 A gardener at the Royal Botanic Gardens, Kew in London, Alexander confesses to a disproportionate affection for the English country garden; its wonderful balance of structure and exuberance is the reason he's never moved abroad, even though he loves to travel to different countries in search of botanical beauty. His gardening career blossomed early when, at the age of 13, he got a job as a garden boy at a manor house in his home village in the Cotswolds.

Alexander says: *"Always consider the size and use-value of the space available; think about light and aspect and choose plants that will thrive in those specific conditions."*

> ❝ *I like to have something in flower every week of the year, which takes careful planning.*

Anders

📷 **@arcticgardener**

🙂 **Anders Røyneberg, 38, Norwegian**

📍 **Oslo, Norway**

As a psychiatric nurse, Anders is a big believer in the therapeutic benefits of plant care and its positive effects on mental health. With a 10-year old orange tree that's grown so tall it towers over him, he's an aspirational 'plant dad', boasting a collection of over 100 plants that are all thriving in his home.

Anders says: "*I always say that plant people are friendly people; the plant community is so supportive and creative and we all want a greener world both indoors and outdoors. I hope I can inspire people to live greener—it really is easy, even if you live in a cold place like Norway.*"

> ❝ *If you're starting out, choose plants that are easy to care for, like succulents with thick, green leaves.*

Ben

📷 **@bennguyendesign**

👦 **Nguyen Vinh Hien, 28, Vietnamese**

📍 **Tokyo, Japan**

ⓘ Even though Ben is an interior stylist, he doesn't place his plants in his apartment according to appearance alone; instead, he moves his plants around to the best spots to keep them happy, whether that's a table, a wall or a ceiling. But that doesn't mean he forgets about the visual. Ben is a keen painter, and likes to paint his pots in a mix of patterns and colors to give each plant its own style.

Ben says: *"We all start from somewhere and learn along the way. There might be times when your plants die, some of mine did too, but that is how I learned—so don't be discouraged. I am grateful to have found a community of plant lovers on Instagram and YouTube. Reading and listening to everyone's tips helps me a lot."*

❝ *No one is born a pro at plant caring.*

Bernat

@bernatamate

Bernat Amate, 24, Spanish

Spain, Barcelona

Bernat inherited his fondness for plants from his grandmother, who keeps a huge collection of *Alocasias* in the family beach house. An interior designer, Bernat describes his plant styling as casual and impulsive. He's also got a penchant for pots. When he spies one he loves, he'll rush home with it and experiment to see which plant fits it best.

Bernat says: *"Plant collections are very personal, but if you don't have a large space, don't accumulate hundreds of tiny plants. Your plants should shine as the central focus in the room—always look for a general harmony of space."*

> " *Choose your plants and pots well, and place them carefully.*

Blendi

📷 **@balajblendi**

👦 **Blendi Balaj, 25, Albanian**

📍 **Berlin, Germany**

ⓘ Blendi doesn't like to pick a favorite plant—because he loves all plants equally. He attributes this love to growing up surrounded by plants and flowers, courtesy of his green-thumb parents. He likes to follow their example by having a thriving garden in his home. He's particularly grateful for this urban jungle whenever he has a bad day at work or doesn't sleep well, as being surrounded by plants makes him feel alive and happy.

Blendi says: *"Try to understand what your plants need. I only water and put my plants in the sun when I feel they need it."*

“ *The clearest way into the universe is through an indoor garden.*

Bryson

📷 **@brysonjmosley**

👦 **Bryson Jay Mosley, 29, American**

📍 **Portland, Oregon, USA**

ⓘ Bryson is a salesman who has learned to always see the sunny side of plant care. He doesn't fret too much if he loses a plant, as he recognizes it's all part of a learning process. He's also got a great tip for growing plants in a hot climate: ice cubes! Every two days or so, he feeds a few to his favorite plants in between waterings to keep them from dehydrating in the summer heat.

Bryson says: *"When you're looking for new plants, check out the local secondhand sales websites. I got all my favorite plants cheaply from someone who had to give them up."*

❝ *Everyone has killed or lost plants. Find the type of plants that work best for you and roll with it!*

Budi

@darmawandii

👦 **Budi Darmawan, 28, Indonesian**

📍 **Jakarta, Indonesia**

ⓘ Budi owns a coffee shop and prides himself on keeping his customers, like his plants, happy and hydrated. He points out that you shouldn't forget to feed your plants (give them some manure if you really want to treat them) and remember that fresh water is important for maintaining that green glow. He's also a keen adventurer, and an indefatigable optimist. His signature hashtag is "don't forget to be happy".

Budi says: *"Plants need to be looked after and I feed and water mine every morning and every evening. To hydrate them through the night I put some ice cubes in with my plants; this helps the soil absorb the water evenly."*

> " *Plants are like human beings to me! They demand the same attention.*

Cody

📷 **@codyraptorowens**

👦 **Cody Owens, 28, American**

📍 **South Pasadena, California, USA**

ⓘ Cody is a hands-on plant dad who believes that showering your plants with love and affection is the best thing you can do to raise a healthy indoor garden. Cody, who works in an artisan ice-cream shop, has diverse taste in plants; his favorites include moon cacti, rubber plants, and *Monstera deliciosa*.

Cody says: *"I honestly think that if you treat your plants like they are your babies, you will all live a happy life. Love them, hug them, kiss them, miss them. Get together for dinner, call them by their names, be the plant dad you were meant to be."*

❝ *Let your plants be very independent. I often let them style themselves.*

Corentin

📷 **@corentinpfeifferfleuriste**

👦 **Corentin Pfeiffer, 27, French**

📍 **Paris, France**

ⓘ An artisan florist, Corentin is skilled in the art of flower arrangement. When he's not crafting constellations of petals, he likes to tend to his family of ferns—an unusual species of plant, which, if you didn't know, reproduces neither by flowers nor seeds but instead via spores.

Corentin says: *"A little bit of love and passion are my secrets. Plants are living beings, and just as we need to be cared for, so do they. Take care of them every day, watering them, observing them, nurturing them, cleaning them ... But most importantly, make sure you treat them with love."*

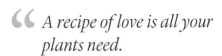

A recipe of love is all your plants need.

Cory

📷 **@corypaul2**

👦 **Cory Paul Jarrell, 28, American**

📍 **Portland, Oregon, USA**

💬 Nerding out about plants is one of Cory's favorite hobbies. He's a trained horticulturist at Portland's delightful wholesale house plant store, The Potted Elephant, and he tends to collect weird-looking plants like *Aroids*, *Rhipsalis paradoxa*, and *Aloe aculeata*. His garden may look like a science experiment, but it's all in the name of finding out more about the magic of plants.

Cory says: *"Less is more! It is easy to over-care for a plant. Most of them thrive on neglect. If your plant does begin to look like it needs some more affection, research the symptoms and decide what to do systematically. Plants are resilient."*

❝ *I am very interested in the art of bonsai and training plants to achieve a certain aesthetic.*

Dabito

📷 **@dabito**

👦 **Dabito, 34, Asian-American**

📍 **Los Angeles, California, USA**

💬 Dabito is an art director with an appetite for color and variety. His Instagram posts explode with vibrancy, and plants are a big part of how he adds life to interior spaces. One of his favorite ways to display his plants is to create a multifunctional wall desk unit that can double up as a plant showcase and a workspace!

Dabito says: *"I love to give my plant babies baths. It helps to keep their leaves clean of any dirt that has built up, which can block them from absorbing light. When it comes to styling, I love a good plant stand. You can also style plants on books, hang them in a corner, or just have one big statement plant in your room."*

" *If space is an issue, go vertical with plants! I love the look of living walls.*

Emil

📷 **@thelimelife_**

👦 **Emil Lime, 32, South African–Indian**

📍 **Cape Town, South Africa**

💬 As a graphic designer and photographer, Emil has an eye for attractive plants. His favorite plants are the peace lily and rubber plant, which are known for their big, bountiful and beautiful leaves. For Emil, it's all about matching the plant to the space. Once you've done that, you need to find the right pot!

Emil says: *"I used to kill my plants until I learned not to overwater."*

❝ *The most important thing is to love your plants.*

Glenn

📷 **@glenn.arvor**

👦 **Glenn Arvor, 35, French**

📍 **Sydney, New South Wales, Australia**

💬 As you might guess from the statuesque combinations of plant, flower and form that furnish his Instagram feed, Glenn is a boutique florist, one who elevates flower arrangement to an art form. He loves to create textured combinations—arabesques of height and depth—and he always strives to avoid making bouquets that will look static.

Glenn says: *"Care involves understanding your plant material—succulents, for instance, do not require a lot of water but do need sunlight, while delicate ferns need a constant water supply, semi shade and protection from the frost."*

" *My favorite plant? Impossible to say. I love anything that captures my imagination.*

Goof

📷 **@goofkloosterman**

🧒 **Goof Kloosterman, 28, Dutch**

📍 **Utrecht, Netherlands**

💬 Visual artist Goof treats his plants as family, which means that he doesn't like to pick a favorite—even though he has a soft spot for his 16-year-old *Austrocylindropuntia subulata*, otherwise known as Eve's needle cactus. The cactus was the first plant Goof bought, and it's still growing strong, creating weird and curvey shapes with its branches. This is just what Goof enjoys; he likes plants that grow wild, and wants to be surrounded by an indoor garden of diverse plants.

Goof says: *"I completely rely on my gut feeling when it comes to taking care of plants, I don't use rules or systems. I just see or feel if the plant needs caring. Try a lot of different plants and see which ones really become a friend to you and your house. I have adopted a lot of sad plants from friends and gave away unhappy ones that didn't match me."*

> " *Try to see if there is a plant exchange community around or set one up with friends.*

Igor

📷 **@igorjosif**

👦 **Igor Josifovic, 39, Austrian**

📍 **Munich, Germany**

ⓘ Not only does Igor run @urbanjungle, a prominent Instagram account dedicated to the green life, he also maintains a popular interior design blog. So he really knows what he's talking about when he stresses the importance of picking a plant that will become part of your home, lifestyle, and daily routine. Don't pick a plant just because it looks good!

Igor says: *"I try to keep a regular plant care routine and turn it into some extra me-time. I love to play with various planters for extra visual impact. I also do pottery and create my own planters from time to time."*

66 *Make plants your friends, not foes.*

James B

📷 **@baetanical**

🧑 **James Barela, 29, American**

📍 **Austin, Texas, USA**

ⓘ As a ceramicist, James knows how to spot a good pot. His advice is to marry the plant's forms, textures, and colors with your chosen receptacle: trailing plants tend to look nice in broad, shallow pots, whereas a plant with some height will look eye-catching when growing in a tall, thinner vessel. When James isn't designing graphics or ceramics, he is documenting his adventures in plant care on his blog, Baetanical.

James says: *"I employ a 'survival of the fittest' approach to caring for plants. If I try a plant and it doesn't seem to like the conditions I'm able to provide, I like to swap it out instead of trying to imitate the conditions it naturally grows in."*

❝ *Growing plants doesn't have to be hard as long as you find ones that thrive naturally in your space.*

James I

📷 **@jamesipy**

👦 **James Ip, 50, Singaporean**

📍 **Singapore**

ⓘ After a day at the office, IT manager James comes home to an oasis of luxuriant green. His favorite plants include maidenhair and staghorn ferns, although these herbaceous shade-lovers wilt and complain in direct sunlight, something James has to watch out for in tropical Singapore. But he places these plants around a cute mini indoor pond to keep them happy.

James says: *"Make full use of your vertical space by introducing hanging plants: the area near a window is the perfect opportunity. Visualizing the room like a canvas lets you hang the plants at different lengths, and you can play with different shapes and textures, mixing plants with leaves that point up with those that hang down."*

❝ *Whenever I'm traveling, I love to visit the local botanical gardens and plant nurseries.*

Jamie

📷 **@jamies_jungle**

👦 **Jamie Song, 36, Taiwanese**

📍 **London, United Kingdom**

ⓘ As an art dealer, Jamie knows a few things about creating the perfect canvas for his plants. He features a lot of hanging varieties in his home, adding drama to his high ceilings. He displays his floor plants on vintage stands of different heights to create a visual tapestry. The most important part of an attractive urban garden is making sure your plants stay healthy, so Jamie dedicates a Sunday every few weeks to caring for his plants, repotting, trimming, and watering them.

Jamie says: *"My favorite plant is my* Aglaonema pictum, *which my mom went through a lot of trouble to bring from Taiwan. It has the most beautiful camouflage pattern on its leaves; I couldn't find one in Europe. She had to obtain a phytosanitary certificate and carry it bare-rooted on the plane and declare it at UK customs."*

> ❝ *An ordinary but healthy plant will bring infinitely more pleasure than a trendy but struggling plant. Keep the type of plants suitable for the conditions of your home—don't force it.*

Jan K

📷 **@homebyfousna**

🧑 **Jan Komárek, 34, Czech**

📍 **Bogotà, Colombia**

ⓘ Jan is an adventurous soul, and whenever he goes off on his travels, he returns from the trip with a new cutting to nurture at home. Caring for indoor plants can be tricky in Colombia: though the climate maintains a perfect level of humidity, Bogota's high altitude means afternoon sunlight can be toxic. But with a little careful attention, Jan maintains a beautiful living wall of lush green vines.

Jan says: *"There's always space for a new plant. Still, you don't have to go crazy and buy dozens of plants just to create an 'urban jungle'. Keep it simple and remember that your plants will grow and take up more space as time goes on. Also, go easy on the watering: it's the number one cause of death for my plants."*

> ❝ *I don't like plastic materials. I house most of my plants in handmade plain terracotta pots.*

Jan R

📷 **@jarobin_**

🧒 **Jan Robin, 30, Slovenian**

📍 **Maribor, Slovenia**

ⓘ You might expect a chemist to be particular about his watering schedule, but Jan is self-avowedly more of a go-with-the-flow type person who trusts his instincts. Having built up his own domestic jungle, he loves spreading the plant love by decorating his friends' interiors—often by giving away little plantlets that he has propagated, which make intimate presents for his nearest and dearest.

Jan says: *"My house plants are so much more than just decorations to me; they are my friends, my inspiration. An apartment without plants is like a person without a personality."*

> ❝ *I hope that the future brings me a huge house, with big windows and lots of space, so I can fill it with plants.*

John

📷 **@delapa1**

👦 **Dr John de la Parra, 38, American**

📍 **Boston, Massachusetts, USA**

ℹ️ John is a phytochemist, which means he studies the chemicals that can be derived from plants and is intimate with the biological specifics of his favorite greenery. At the moment, he is studying the medicinal plants used by indigenous people all over the world, testing to see whether their unique molecular makeup might hold miraculous treatments for neglected diseases.

John says: *"If you have trouble growing plants indoors but really want the simple beauty of lush green foliage, here is one great solution: buy ten bushy pots of indestructible devil's ivy, otherwise known as* Epipremnum aureum, *and place them around your home. Beware though—they are toxic if ingested. Keep them away from pets and children."*

> ❝ *To me, plants are integral to both our sacred and scientific understanding of the world.*

Jon

📷 **@jongomezdelap**

👦 **Jon Gómes de la Peña, 33, Spanish**

📍 **Barcelona, Spain**

ⓘ Jon doesn't spend a lot of time planning his green family—he falls in love with plants on first sight and brings them home. His existing plants are always accepting of these arrivals, and together they create a new harmony. As an audiovisual creator, Jon loves plants that create a big visual impact, and his favorites include the pink flowering *Bougainvillea*, *Monstera deliciosa* and all kinds of ferns.

Jon says: *"I spray water on their leaves regularly and use vitamins. I also talk to them and sing empowering ballads!"*

> " *When I feel like I want a plant in my family, it's already decided.*

Jonathan

📷 **@jrlefrancois**

🧑 **Jonathan Lefrançois, 32, Canadian**

📍 **Montréal, Quebec, Canada**

ⓘ A graphic designer by trade, Jonathan has always kept his home quite minimalist, but recently the plants have taken over! Jonathan has a soft spot for his variegated *Monstera*, which was his first plant purchase, but he also loves more underappreciated, easy-to-care-for plants, like snake plants. He recommends plants as a hobby—but don't buy too many at once, or you'll be overwhelmed!

Jonathan says: *"I think it's important to pace yourself and get to know the fundamentals of plant care before you get too carried away. I mostly rely on plant trading groups online to get new additions. Not only do you get access to new varieties but also you meet new folks with common interests."*

> ❝ *For anyone wanting to grow their collection, plant trading groups are the best way!*

Jono

📷 **@jono.fleming**

🧒 **Jono Fleming, 30, Australian**

📍 **Sydney, New South Wales, Australia**

ℹ️ Jono wears his love of plants on his sleeve; he has his favorite plant, the native Australian *Corymbia ficifolia*, tattooed on his arm. His love of plants also extends to his home, which Jono has turned into an urban jungle, and to his job as a style editor. Jono often adds a bit of greenery to his photo shoots—and sometimes he even gets to take these plants home at the end of a shoot.

Jono says: *"I used to struggle with my plants until I realized that I was buying the wrong type for my home environment. Make sure you know how much light, sun, water, and attention your plants will need; from there you can put together the perfect urban jungle and proudly boast a green thumb."*

> ❝ *I choose low maintenance plants that require little water but reap huge rewards.*

Luca

👦 **Luca Iacovene, 26, Italian**

📍 **Rome, Italy**

ⓘ Luca is a philosophy student and when he isn't learning about existential conundrums he's reading up on how to look after his *Ginkgo biloba*— an ancient specimen of plant so old that it was young 270 million years ago. He consults plant expert friends and buys specialist books to ensure he knows as much as possible about plant care.

Luca says: *"When it comes to plants, less isn't more! Especially when you combine your plants with stacks of books, or arrange them in unusual spaces like the bathroom or the kitchen."*

❝ *Bring on the plant invasion!*

Mark

@mrk.gif

[face icon] **Mark Cameron, 28, Canadian**

[location icon] **Toronto, Ontario, Canada**

[info icon] A graphic designer, Mark also likes to try his hand at interior design—a fun, though potentially expensive hobby. But plants make for beautiful and affordable decoration, and he'd recommend filling rooms with greenery to everyone. His favorite plant changes daily: mainly he's just an advocate of planty profusion.: the more the merrier! He points out that looking after one plant is not that different to looking after twenty of them—so go on, buy another.

Mark says: *"I have a pretty tight watering schedule, but it takes more than that to get your plants to thrive. Playing music for them, providing them with egg shells, using carbonated water—it all adds up to happy plants."*

> *" Plants like plant friends, so make sure everybody's got a buddy!*

Martin

📷 **@martinehmele**

👦 **Martin Ehmele, 28, German**

📍 **Vienna, Austria**

ⓘ The best thing about working from home for Martin, who is a marketing manager and freelance writer, is that he gets to spend time with his plants, including favorites such as his *Monstera delicosa*, calatheas, and rubber plants. He likes to spend his breaks watering and caring for his verdant indoor garden, and he finds it easy to let his plants entice him away from his computer screen. But he's careful not to over-water!

Martin says: *"The number one killer of house plants is over-watering, which leads to root rot. Don't let your plants sit in water and don't automatically water all your house plants on a schedule."*

> ❝ *If you're dating a person who has plastic plants at home, run!*

Maurício

@maujorge

😊 **Maurício Jorge, 31, Brazilian**

📍 **São Paulo, Brazil**

ⓘ Furniture designer Maurício likes to get out into nature and find new waterfalls whenever he can—so it's only natural that when it comes to his plants, he wants them to grow wild. For his favorite plants, such as *Philodendron martianum* and his *Monstera deliciosa*, Maurício says no to pruning sheers, but yes to regular watering and a monthly dose of fertilizer.

Maurício says: *"Make sure your room has adequate lighting for the plant that you want. If you are the type of person who forgets your obligations, choose plants that require little water."*

" *Talk to the plants, it will do them and you well.*

Mert

📷 **@mrtzldg**

🙂 **Mert Ozuludag, 30, Turkish**

📍 **Izmir, Turkey**

ⓘ It would be hard to say what Mert's friends and fans on Instagram like more—his verdant plant collection or his adorable pet pug. Mert enjoys nothing better than making himself a cup of coffee and drinking it surrounded by his plants and pet family. Once Mert has finished his coffee, he doesn't throw the grounds in the trash. Instead he uses them to feed his growing urban garden.

Mert says: *"My morning ritual is drinking a cup of coffee surrounded by my plants. It makes me energetic for the rest of the day!"*

66 *Don't throw coffee grounds away; use them as plant manure.*

Michael

📷 **@houseofhortus**

👦 **Michael Madjus, 36, Canadian**

📍 **Toronto, Ontario, Canada**

ℹ️ Michael is a plant-obsessed creative. He dabbles in everything from photography to ceramics, illustration to fashion and furniture, and finds ways to incorporate his green thumb into all his artistic pursuits. Living in a four-season city like Toronto has its challenges: his plants need extra attention in winter in particular. As a designer, he finds plant caring and plant styling go hand in hand. Where a plant looks good is as important as where it will grow well, if you want to create a beautiful living décor.

Michael says: *"Every home and office can benefit from a plant or two (or three or four!). With a myriad of house plant species to choose from, there's a plant for everyone and for every space. Remember, every indoor jungle started off with a single plant."*

❝ *Some of my favorite plants are not super fancy or expensive, but those to which I have some kind of emotional tie.*

Mihalis

⸻

📷 **@mihalisnyc**

👦 **Mihalis Petrou, 27, Cypriot**

📍 **New York City, USA**

ⓘ Mihalis is a passionate floral stylist and gardener who says an emphatic NO to fake foliage—don't do it! He really treasures his plants; their care and comfort have helped him manage his mental health and he nurtures a colorful range of cacti, succulents, and purple-leaved beauties, as well as a characterful and fragrant snail vine.

Mihalis says: *"I wake up to 15 plants in my bedroom. They're all fairly small, the biggest being a 30-centimeter* Pachira, *and the smallest a two-inch* Kalanchoe orgyalis. *To keep them healthy, I use a humidifier and even regularly take them in the shower to give their leaves a good clean."*

> " *In this household, styling plants is not a priority; their beauty is greatest in a simple clay or glass pot.*

Muhammed

[📷] **@behind_the_seeds**

[👦] **Muhammed Osman, 36, Egyptian**

[📍] **Cairo, Egypt**

[ℹ️] Muhammed is a vet, but he doesn't just look after animals— he's a pro protector of more than 150 plants! His routine is dedicated: he mists daily with a portable steamer, and Saturday is "plant gym" day, when all the showering, re-potting, fertilizing, trimming, and propagating takes place. A similar conscientiousness characterizes his attention to styling: his planters are a uniform white so nothing distracts the eye from the detailed beauty of each plant's leaves.

Muhammed says: *"Light! If there is one word that unlocks the secret of healthy plants, it's light. I believe that correct lighting is the solution to your watering worries and will mean the right growth pattern. Knowing your plant's light requirements is crucial."*

> *I'm in love with green plants. They give me the jungle vibes I need.*

Mykie

📷 **@mykier**

👦 **Mykie Rogers, 36, American**

📍 **Los Angeles, California, USA**

ⓘ Mykie is an art director and outdoor enthusiast. Often found hiking through the hills exploring Mother Nature's nooks and crannies, he keeps some of the wilderness alive in his own apartment with a collection of his favorite prickly friends, cacti, along with other beautiful leafy green things.

Mykie says: *"Looking after plants isn't complicated: they're no different from any other living thing. Give them the basics: water, food, light, and shelter."*

" *Treat your plants like your babies. Sing, talk and nurture them, and they will grow, grow, grow!*

Nick

📷 **@nickotene**

👦 **Nick Stefanovic, 23, Irish**

📍 **Dublin, Ireland**

💬 Nick thinks it's important to always seize new opportunities, and remember to take the time to have fun and relax. He applies the same attitude to his favorite plants, which are a diverse mix from all over the globe, including kangaroo paw from Australia, *Pilea peperomioides* from China, and *Sedum burrito* from Mexico. As a medical student, Nick likes to keep people and plants healthy; for his plants, Nick believes that some all-purpose fertilizer goes a long way.

Nick says: *"Learn how to propagate your plants! The only thing better than one plant that you love is two or three. You can gift them to friends and family for a nice personal touch."*

❝ *You feel great when the little plants grow happily.*

Olle

📷 **@upleafting**

😊 **Olle Eriksson, 29, Swedish**

📍 **Malmö, Sweden**

ⓘ Photographer and plant consultant Olle has a soft spot for challenging plants, as well as ones that look a little, well, weird—including the *Philodendron squamiferum*, which is furry with funny-shaped leaves. The bulk of his collection are tropical varieties, which are more demanding and showy with their huge leafy foliage.

Olle says: *"Try to find out the real names of your plants as it's great to know this when searching for tips and care instructions. If you suspect the name from the store is incorrect, try taking a photo of your plant and doing a reverse image search online. Or just send it to me! I'll help you out."*

> ❝ *It's never too late to become a plant addict.*

Oskar

📷 **@plantthatplant**

🙂 **Oskar Widmark, 25, Swedish**

📍 **Skåne, Lund, Sweden**

💬 When asked what his favorite plant is, Oskar said it is currently a *Chelone oblique*: a perennial with pink turtle-like flowers that make a "plantastic" contrast to its serious name. A landscape architecture student with a mischievous sense of humor, he's a cheerful "plant petter"—it gets rid of dust, which can block pores.

Oskar says: *"Just started your plant journey? Big congrats, and welcome to the family! I worried about watering correctly when I first started. A rule of thumb when watering your loved ones is to let them dry out before you drench them. You can save them from drying out but it's much harder to save them from drowning."*

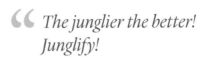

❝ *The junglier the better! Junglify!*

Patrick

📷 **@copperplants**

👦 **Patrick Jung, 27, German**

📍 **Kaiserslautern, Germany**

💬 Patrick is a plant scientist, or, to be more technical, a cryptobotanist. He's so fascinated by plants he is studying them for his PhD, investigating how miraculous lichens are able to survive in the most extreme ecosystems on Earth, like the Atacama Desert and Antarctica. With his extensive knowledge of biology, we can assume his plants are not only well loved, but superlatively well looked after!

Patrick says: *"Don't be afraid to shift your plants' positions. Changing perspective isn't just good for people, you know!"*

> ❝ *I care for and style my favorite plants with a lot of love and patience.*

Pierluigi

📷 **@hyperdecadence**

🧒 **Pierluigi Fracassi, 36, Italian**

📍 **Madrid, Spain**

💬 Pierluigi is a creative director and artist who draws inspiration from nature, even though he lives in the heart of a thriving metropolis. But before he was a city boy, Pierluigi grew up in a small village in the middle of the mountains in Italy, where his grandmother, Cloridea, taught him to grow, respect, and take care of plants. He has a huge love for the natural world, which always reminds him of his grandmother, and particularly loves luscious and fruitful plants like the common fig tree.

Pierluigi says: *"I name my plants. I don't see them as part of the furniture to make our house look good, but as part of the family."*

" *Caring for plants is all about having respect for nature.*

Raymond

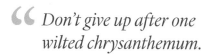

📷 **@mustybooks**

👦 **Raymond Carter, 35, American**

📍 **Garnet Valley, Pennsylvania, USA**

💬 As a horticulturist, Raymond isn't afraid to be bold with his plant selection. His favorites are the ancient cycads, as well as leafy begonias. But he doesn't restrict himself to just these two plants. Raymond views his home as a living canvas, one he paints with a wide variety of plants spanning dozens of genera.

Raymond says: *"It is not uncommon for people to message me saying, 'I wish I could live in a world like yours.' What I tell them is that we all live in the same world, and plants are virtually everywhere. There is no such thing as a green thumb, only those with the willingness to learn from their mistakes and the patience to help things grow."*

66 *Don't give up after one wilted chrysanthemum.*

Remigiusz

[camera icon] **@warsawjungle**

[face icon] **Remigiusz Zawadzki, 35, Polish**

[location icon] **Warsaw, Poland**

[info icon] A music producer and sound engineer, Remek is interested in how his twin obsessions relate: is music good for plant growth? The evidence suggests that music isn't great for plant growth—it might, in fact, stress plants out! But if you do want to play music to your green family, classical and jazz are the best choices.

Remek says: *"You shouldn't choose plants just for their looks. You should also think about their needs. Will they survive in the environment you can offer them? Will they suit your temperament?"*

> *If you're a forgetful person, it's probably kindest to go for a cactus!*

Ronnie

📷 **@ohsummossum**

👦 **Ronnie Khoo, 35, Malaysian**

📍 **Kuala Lumpur, Malaysia**

ℹ️ Ronnie loves the artistic expression of creating a terrarium so much that he now shares the joy of building these miniature plant kingdoms with others as a full-time job. When constructing his own terrariums, Ronnie picks plants that do well in jars, like mosses, aquatic plants, and small tropical plants. He likes to see them show off their personalities as they evolve.

Ronnie says: *"Terrariums are not static decoration; they grow and change over time. Like all gardens, terrariums will benefit from regular tending, allowing us to observe how small plants interact together like they do in the wild. I like recreating a natural look so my designs usually feature asymmetrical placements and lush textures, and look better once the plants are grown in."*

> ❝ *Plants reveal themselves at their own slower pace, so discovering their secrets always feels like an achievement because it takes time.*

Shabi

📷 **@fiori_tlv**

🧒 **Sagi Samila, 33, Israeli**

📍 **Tel Aviv, Israel**

ⓘ It's hard not to feel envious of Shabi, who spends his days surrounded by plants and flowers. He runs a specialty flower shop in Tel Aviv, where he can let his imagination run wild creating bouquets and arrangements that bring joy to all of his customers. Apart from his floral friends, Shabi loves big green plants, although he has a soft spot for small cacti and succulents.

Shabi says: *"I like to create magic with plants. I try to arrange the plants and products in my shop to make a harmonious space that's full of style!"*

❝ *The best way to care for your plants is to watch them closely, and decide what each individual plant needs— whether that's fertilizer, water, sun, or shade.*

Thiago

📷 **@thiagovicenteoliveira**

👦 **Thiago Vicente de Oliveira, 31, Brazilian**

📍 **Lisbon, Portugal**

ⓘ As a model, Thiago understands what it takes to make sure you're looking your best and he assumes the same responsibility for his plants—they get a weekly clean to keep them gorgeous and green. They're also his spiritual companions: their slow growth and essential natural beauty remind him daily that it's what's on the inside that counts.

Thiago says: *"I'm captivated by all my plants, but I have to confess the tropical ones are my favorites because they remind me of home. I look after all of them every day and give each one individual attention."*

> ❝ *I treat my plants as if they were my daughters! I give them care, food, water, and lots of love.*

Travis

ⓘ Paramedic Travis has turned his home in San Francisco into a tropical plant paradise. While it's not easy to mimic a humid Mediterranean climate in the dry heat of California, Travis has perfected his routine of constantly rinsing and misting his plants to help them thrive. He's not a man to be put off by a challenge, as evidenced by his affection for plants in the *Tillandsia* genus, commonly known as air plants, which have particular care requirements as they have no roots.

Travis says: *"When creating a garden in dense, urban settings your available space is typically limited. Mount specimens to walls or fences, grow species that will climb or hang overhead, or create an 'air garden' with* tillandsias, bromeliads, and orchids.*"*

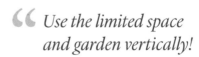

" *Use the limited space and garden vertically!*

Tyrell

📷 **@gothaigo**

👦 **Tyrell Gough, 27, Canadian**

📍 **Toronto, Ontario, Canada**

💬 When Tyrell, a fashion photographer, isn't shooting portraits, you'll most likely find him at home relaxing in his tropical jungle. Replete with lush foliage and vibrant hues, this mini rainforest provides a "get-away experience" after a long day's work. Though he is fond of all tropical plants, if he had to pick a favorite, it would be the *Guzmania lingulata*. He loves its striking scarlet star and metallic green spear-shaped leaves.

Tyrell says: *Having plants can change the atmosphere of any room, but knowing how to care for them is essential. I researched the characteristics of each of my plants to make sure I knew their ideal temperature and humidity, the best watering routine, and how often I should fertilize them.*

> " *If you already have a few plants in your living space, you should get more. If you don't have any at all, get some! I highly recommend it.*

Zack

📷 **@zack_bez**

👤 **Zacarias Bezunartea, 42, American**

📍 **Brooklyn, New York, USA**

💬 As a Chief Operating Officer, Zack leads a busy life but at least he can put all the coffee he drinks to good use, as he shares it with his banana plant! He and his favorite shrub also enjoy listening to NPR together, and Zack finds time to sing to the rest of his plant pets, as well as indulging them, when they need attention, with some fertilizer or a new pot.

Zack says: *The most helpful tip I ever read said to know as much as possible about a plant's native environment and keep that in mind when caring for it. I usually look into that when I first get a plant. But if, after a while, a plant doesn't seem happy or struggles with me I just move on and give it away.*

> ❝ *It's sort of like dating. If we don't click, then why force it?*

Zaki

@zqqyjml

👦 **Zaki Jamil, 25, Singaporean**

📍 **Singapore**

💬 Some people love soap operas for the drama, but Zaki prefers the natural drama that occurs in the plant kingdom. This Singaporean horticulturalist and landscape designer loves plants with big leaves and even bigger personalities, like the breadfruit tree, *Ficus dammaropsis*, *Dillenias*, *Agaves* and palm trees. His plants never fail to lift his mood, particularly when they are placed in white- and earth-toned pots, a styling move he highly recommends because they go well with everything!

Zaki says: *"I enjoy kicking back and observing my plants sway in the wind. To break up uniformity and add contrasting textures, I match big-leafed plants like* Alocasias *and* Philodendrons *with palms that have finer leaves. I also enjoy experimenting unconventional styles, such as mixing tropical plants with arid plants like* Agaves, Yuccas *and* Aloes.*"*

> ❝ *Don't be afraid to place different plants together! You never know how it might turn out. Mixing them together can bring out the best of their textures and colors.*

First published in Great Britain in 2019 by Elwin Street Productions

First published in the United States of America in 2019 by Chronicle Books LLC

Copyright © Elwin Street Productions Limited 2018
Conceived and produced by
Elwin Street Productions Limited
14 Clerkenwell Green
London EC1R 0DP
www.elwinstreet.com

Library of Congress Cataloging-in-Publication Data available.

ISBN 978-1-4521-7444-0

Manufactured in China.

Cover design by Scott Cain, Monkeyfern

Photograph of John (pp.56–57) by Ernest Anemone; of Remigiusz (pp.92–93) by Beata Malyska; of Mykie (pp.80–81) by Randy Rosario; and of Igor (pp.44–45) by Jules Villbrandt. All other photographs supplied by and used by permission of the boys.

Chronicle Books LLC
680 Second Street
San Francisco, CA 94107

www.chroniclebooks.com

10 9 8 7 6 5 4 3 2 1